# Adult

# MAD LIBS®

*World's Greatest Word Game*

# ADVICE FOR THE LOVELORN MAD LIBS

By Roger Price and Leonard Stern

*PSS!*
PRICE STERN SLOAN

ROADSIDE AMUSEMENTS
an imprint of
CHAMBERLAIN BROS.
Published by the Penguin Group
Price Stern Sloan, a division of Penguin Group for Young Readers.
Penguin Group (USA) Inc., 375 Hudson Street, New York, New York 10014, USA
Penguin Group (Canada), 10 Alcorn Avenue, Toronto, Ontario, Canada M4V 3B2
(a division of Pearson Penguin Canada Inc.)
Penguin Books Ltd, 80 Strand, London WC2R 0RL, England
Penguin Ireland, 25 St Stephen's Green, Dublin 2, Ireland (a division of Penguin Books Ltd)
Penguin Group (Australia), 250 Camberwell Road, Camberwell, Victoria 3124, Australia
(a division of Pearson Australia Group Pty Ltd)
Penguin Books India Pvt Ltd, 11 Community Centre, Panchsheel Park,
New Delhi-110 017, India
Penguin Group (NZ), Cnr Airborne and Rosedale Roads,
Albany, Auckland 1310, New Zealand (a division of Pearson New Zealand Ltd)
Penguin Books (South Africa) (Pty) Ltd, 24 Sturdee Avenue,
Rosebank, Johannesburg 2196, South Africa

Penguin Books Ltd, Registered Offices: 80 Strand, London WC2R 0RL, England

An application has been submitted to register this book with the Library of Congress.

ISBN 1-59609-152-5

Printed in the United States of America
10  9  8  7  6  5  4  3  2

# MAD LIBS®
## INSTRUCTIONS

MAD LIBS® is a game for people who don't like games!
It can be played by one, two, three, four, or forty.

### • RIDICULOUSLY SIMPLE DIRECTIONS

In this tablet you will find stories containing blank spaces where words are left out. One player, the READER, selects one of these stories. The READER does not tell anyone what the story is about. Instead, he/she asks the other players, the WRITERS, to give him/her words. These words are used to fill in the blank spaces in the story.

### • TO PLAY

The READER asks each WRITER in turn to call out a word—an adjective or a noun or whatever the space calls for—and uses them to fill in the blank spaces in the story. The result is a MAD LIBS® game.

When the READER then reads the completed MAD LIBS® game to the other players, they will discover that they have written a story that is fantastic, screamingly funny, shocking, silly, crazy, or just plain dumb—depending upon which words each WRITER called out.

### • EXAMPLE (*Before* and *After*)

"_____ !" he said _____
         EXCLAMATION                                     ADVERB

as he jumped into his convertible _____ and
                                                   NOUN

drove off with his _____ wife.
                         ADJECTIVE

"*Ouch!* !" he said *Stupidly*
         EXCLAMATION                                  ADVERB

as he jumped into his convertible *cat* and
                                                  NOUN

drove off with his *brave* wife.
                         ADJECTIVE

# MAD LIBS®
## QUICK REVIEW

In case you have forgotten what adjectives, adverbs, nouns, and verbs are, here is a quick review:

An ADJECTIVE describes something or somebody. *Lumpy, soft, ugly, messy,* and *short* are adjectives.

An ADVERB tells how something is done. It modifies a verb and usually ends in "ly." *Modestly, stupidly, greedily,* and *carefully* are adverbs.

A NOUN is the name of a person, place, or thing. *Sidewalk, umbrella, bridle, bathtub,* and *nose* are nouns.

A VERB is an action word. *Run, pitch, jump,* and *swim* are verbs. Put the verbs in past tense if the directions say PAST TENSE. *Ran, pitched, jumped,* and *swam* are verbs in the past tense.

When we ask for A PLACE, we mean any sort of place: a country or city *(Spain, Cleveland)* or a room *(bathroom, kitchen).*

An EXCLAMATION or SILLY WORD is any sort of funny sound, gasp, grunt, or outcry, like *Wow!, Ouch!, Whomp!, Ick!,* and *Gadzooks!*

When we ask for specific words, like a NUMBER, a COLOR, an ANIMAL, or a PART OF THE BODY, we mean a word that is one of those things, like *seven, blue, horse,* or *head.*

When we ask for a PLURAL, it means more than one. For example, *cat* pluralized is *cats.*

MAD LIBS® is fun to play with friends, but you can also play it by yourself! To begin with, DO NOT look at the story on the page below. Fill in the blanks on this page with the words called for. Then, using the words you have selected, fill in the blank spaces in the story.

Now you've created your own hilarious MAD LIBS® game!

# THE PERFECT BOYFRIEND

NOUN _____

NOUN _____

VERB _____

NUMBER _____

ADJECTIVE_____

ADJECTIVE_____

ADJECTIVE_____

PLURAL NOUN _____

VERB ENDING IN "ING" _____

VERB _____

ADJECTIVE_____

NOUN _____

NOUN _____

NOUN _____

CELEBRITY (MALE)_____

VERB ENDING IN "ING" _____

# MAD LIBS
# THE PERFECT BOYFRIEND

Let's imagine the perfect boyfriend. He would wake you every

morning with a/an _____. He would use his cell
                         NOUN

_____ to_____ you _____ times a day.
      NOUN                  VERB                    NUMBER

He would rub your _____ back after a/an _____
                        ADJECTIVE                          ADJECTIVE

day at the _____office. He would help you shop for
                  ADJECTIVE

_____ without _____ one bit. He
     PLURAL NOUN              VERB ENDING IN "ING"

would _____ all of your friends with his _____
          VERB                                              ADJECTIVE

charm. He would never click over to a pro _____
                                                        NOUN

game while you're watching your favorite episode of

"_____ in the _____." And he wouldn't be
      NOUN                      NOUN

at all jealous of your obsession with _____. Ladies, he is
                                          CELEBRITY (MALE)

out there just _____for you!
                  VERB ENDING IN "ING"

From ADVICE FOR THE LOVELORN MAD LIBS® • Copyright © 2005 by Chamberlain Bros.,
a division of Penguin Group (USA), Inc., 375 Hudson Street, New York, New York 10014.

MAD LIBS® is fun to play with friends, but you can also play it by yourself! To begin with, DO NOT look at the story on the page below. Fill in the blanks on this page with the words called for. Then, using the words you have selected, fill in the blank spaces in the story.

Now you've created your own hilarious MAD LIBS® game!

# ALL SIGNS POINT TO "BREAK UP"

ADJECTIVE_____

ADVERB_____

ADJECTIVE_____

NOUN _____

PART OF THE BODY _____

ADVERB_____

VERB ENDING IN "ING" _____

NOUN _____

PLURAL NOUN _____

ADJECTIVE_____

ADJECTIVE_____

NUMBER _____

CITY _____

SAME NUMBER_____

SAME CITY_____

ADJECTIVE_____

NUMBER _____

ADVERB_____

ADJECTIVE_____

VERB _____

# MAD LIBS®
# ALL SIGNS POINT TO
# "BREAK UP"

Dear Dating Diva,

I have a/an _____ problem. My boyfriend never wants
           ADJECTIVE

to cuddle with me anymore. He's become _____
                                   ADVERB

_____ lately. I've tried having a serious _____
ADJECTIVE                                     NOUN

discussion with him about this problem, but he just turns his

_____ away and ignores me. The other day, I saw this
PART OF THE BODY

couple _____ in a/an _____ and I almost
      VERB ENDING IN "ING"          NOUN

burst into _____. I love this _____ man
         PLURAL NOUN                 ADJECTIVE

and am afraid of becoming a/an _____ spinster if we
                                 ADJECTIVE

break up. What should I do?

—Over _____ in _____
         NUMBER            CITY

Dear _____ in _____,
     SAME NUMBER        SAME CITY

Please reread your _____ letter _____ times. You
              ADJECTIVE         NUMBER

deserve a man who wants to be with you _____. Get rid
                               ADVERB

of this _____ jerk and _____ on with your life.
     ADJECTIVE             VERB

MAD LIBS® is fun to play with friends, but you can also play it by yourself! To begin with, DO NOT look at the story on the page below. Fill in the blanks on this page with the words called for. Then, using the words you have selected, fill in the blank spaces in the story.

Now you've created your own hilarious MAD LIBS® game!

# IT'S OVER!

NAME OF PERSON (MALE)_____

NOUN _____

PLURAL NOUN _____

NOUN _____

PLURAL NOUN _____

NOUN _____

PLURAL NOUN _____

NOUN _____

ADJECTIVE_____

TYPE OF FOOD _____

CELEBRITY (MALE)_____

ADJECTIVE_____

ADJECTIVE_____

ADJECTIVE_____

ADVERB_____

# MAD LIBS®
## IT'S OVER!

Dear _____,
       NAME OF PERSON (MALE)

I know this may come as a _____ you, but it's over.
                         NOUN

I've packed my _____ and am going to stay in a friend's
            PLURAL NOUN

_____tonight. I just cannot be with a man who spends
   NOUN

several _____ in front of a/an _____ mirror
      PLURAL NOUN                   NOUN

every morning, who spends a fortune on _____ and
                                  PLURAL NOUN

clothing, and who spends hours waxing his _____. I
                                   NOUN

can no longer pretend to be interested in _____ears,
                            ADJECTIVE

cold _____, or _____. Our engagement
     TYPE OF FOOD          CELEBRITY (MALE)

is off. I hope you find someone else as _____ as you
                            ADJECTIVE

so that you can both be _____together.
                 ADJECTIVE

_____,
   ADVERB
Me

From ADVICE FOR THE LOVELORN MAD LIBS® • Copyright © 2005 by Chamberlain Bros., a division of Penguin Group (USA), Inc., 375 Hudson Street, New York, New York 10014.

MAD LIBS® is fun to play with friends, but you can also play it by yourself! To begin with, DO NOT look at the story on the page below. Fill in the blanks on this page with the words called for. Then, using the words you have selected, fill in the blank spaces in the story.

Now you've created your own hilarious MAD LIBS® game!

# INDULGE YOURSELF

ADJECTIVE _____

ADJECTIVE _____

ADJECTIVE _____

TYPE OF CONTAINER _____

PLURAL NOUN _____

PLURAL NOUN _____

NOUN _____

ADVERB _____

PLURAL NOUN _____

NUMBER _____

PART OF THE BODY _____

ADJECTIVE _____

VERB _____

VERB _____

PLURAL NOUN _____

VERB _____

ADJECTIVE _____

**ICE CREAM**

# MAD LIBS®
# INDULGE YOURSELF

Don't even try to stay on your _____ diet after a/an
<br>ADJECTIVE

_____ breakup! You now have a really _____
<br>ADJECTIVE                                                   ADJECTIVE

excuse to eat a/an _____ full of chopped
<br>                                TYPE OF CONTAINER

_____ and as many chocolate _____ as
<br>PLURAL NOUN                                      PLURAL NOUN

your _____ desires. What else would go so _____
<br>        NOUN                                       ADVERB

with your viewings of "Desperate _____ _____"?
<br>                                ADJECTIVE      PLURAL NOUN

Who cares if those _____ calories go straight to your
<br>                              NUMBER

_____? You're going through a very _____
<br>PART OF THE BODY                                   ADJECTIVE

time. Plus, you can just _____ to the gym tomorrow
<br>                              VERB

and _____ an extra 30 _____ minutes.
<br>      VERB                              PLURAL NOUN

Who knows, you might _____ the eye of your
<br>                              VERB

_____ soul mate as you _____ on the
<br>ADJECTIVE                                      VERB

StairMaster.

MAD LIBS® is fun to play with friends, but you can also play it by yourself! To begin with, DO NOT look at the story on the page below. Fill in the blanks on this page with the words called for. Then, using the words you have selected, fill in the blank spaces in the story.

Now you've created your own hilarious MAD LIBS® game!

# POST-BREAKUP PURGING

VERB ENDING IN "ING" _____

ADJECTIVE_____

ADJECTIVE_____

CITY _____

ADJECTIVE_____

NUMBER _____

VERB _____

ADJECTIVE_____

ARTICLE OF CLOTHING_____

ADJECTIVE_____

ADJECTIVE_____

NOUN _____

TYPE OF LIQUID _____

ADJECTIVE_____

A PLACE _____

VERB _____

TYPE OF CONTAINER _____

EXCLAMATION_____

VERB ENDING IN "ING" _____

NOUN _____

# MAD LIBS®
# POST-BREAKUP PURGING

Are you still _____ over those _____
VERB ENDING IN "ING"                             ADJECTIVE

photos from your _____ trip to _____
ADJECTIVE                                    CITY

harbor? Have you read and reread the _____ notes he
ADJECTIVE

wrote to you _____ times? Do you still _____
NUMBER                                        VERB

in his _____ _____? It's time to get
ADJECTIVE                ARTICLE OF CLOTHING

over that _____ feeling by tossing all evidence of your
ADJECTIVE

_____ relationship into a big fire (just make sure you
ADJECTIVE

have some _____ nearby in case the flames become
TYPE OF LIQUID

too _____). You could also bury everything in the
ADJECTIVE

_____. Or you can just _____ it in the
A PLACE                                   VERB

_____. _____! You're well on the way
TYPE OF CONTAINER     EXCLAMATION

to _____ him out of your _____!
VERB ENDING IN "ING"                      NOUN

MAD LIBS® is fun to play with friends, but you can also play it by yourself! To begin with, DO NOT look at the story on the page below. Fill in the blanks on this page with the words called for. Then, using the words you have selected, fill in the blank spaces in the story.

Now you've created your own hilarious MAD LIBS® game!

# CLASSIC LOVE LETTER

ADJECTIVE _____

ADJECTIVE _____

VERB _____

NOUN _____

VERB ENDING IN "ING" _____

NOUN _____

VERB _____

PART OF THE BODY (PLURAL) _____

VERB _____

NOUN _____

ADJECTIVE _____

ADJECTIVE _____

PART OF THE BODY _____

NOUN _____

# MAD LIBS®
# CLASSIC LOVE LETTER

Before you start thinking that _____ love doesn't exist,
ADJECTIVE

check out this love _____ letter that Irish writer James
ADJECTIVE

Joyce wrote to his wife, Nora:

My own _____ Nora,
ADJECTIVE

I love you, I cannot _____ without you. . . . I would
VERB

like to go through _____ side by side with you,
NOUN

_____ you more and more until we grew to be one
VERB ENDING IN "ING"

_____ together until the hour should come for us
NOUN

to _____.
VERB

Even now the tears rush to my _____ and sobs
PART OF THE BODY (PLURAL)

_____ my throat as I write this. . . .
VERB

O my _____ be only a little kinder to me, bear with
NOUN

me a little even if I am _____ and _____
ADJECTIVE    ADJECTIVE

and believe me we will be happy together.

Let me have your _____ always close to mine to hear
PART OF THE BODY

every throb of my life, every _____, every joy. —James Joyce
NOUN

MAD LIBS® is fun to play with friends, but you can also play it by yourself! To begin with, DO NOT look at the story on the page below. Fill in the blanks on this page with the words called for. Then, using the words you have selected, fill in the blank spaces in the story.

Now you've created your own hilarious MAD LIBS® game!

# DROWN YOUR SORROWS

ADJECTIVE _____

VERB _____

ADJECTIVE _____

ADJECTIVE _____

PART OF THE BODY _____

NOUN _____

NOUN _____

TYPE OF PLANT _____

TYPE OF ALCOHOL _____

TYPE OF LIQUID _____

ADJECTIVE _____

TYPE OF FRUIT _____

TYPE OF VEGETABLE _____

CELEBRITY DIVA _____

TYPE OF LIQUID _____

ADJECTIVE _____

# MAD LIBS®
# DROWN YOUR SORROWS

Fresh from a/an _____ relationship, you deserve a
                        ADJECTIVE

drink. What better time is there to _____ your libation
                                              VERB

horizons and pick a/an _____ signature "chicktail" to
                              ADJECTIVE

celebrate your freedom? To satisfy your _____ tooth,
                                                  ADJECTIVE

order a Fuzzy _____, a concoction of _____
              PART OF THE BODY                        NOUN

juice and _____ liquor. Or there's the Mojito, made
                  NOUN

with _____, _____, and a splash of
      TYPE OF PLANT          ANOTHER TYPE OF ALCOHOL

_____. If you're in a retro mood, Martinis now come
   TYPE OF LIQUID

in all sorts of _____ varieties. Try a/an _____-tini
                  ADJECTIVE                          TYPE OF FRUIT

or a/an _____-tini. Or maybe a _____,
          TYPE OF VEGETABLE                        CELEBRITY DIVA

libation made with gin and a spritz of _____.
                                            TYPE OF LIQUID

Experiment until you find your most _____ new favorite!
                                          ADJECTIVE

From MAD LIBS® ADVICE FOR THE LOVELORN • Copyright © 2005 by Chamberlain Bros.,
a division of Penguin Group (USA), Inc., New York, 375 Hudson Street, New York, New York 10014.

MAD LIBS® is fun to play with friends, but you can also play it by yourself! To begin with, DO NOT look at the story on the page below. Fill in the blanks on this page with the words called for. Then, using the words you have selected, fill in the blank spaces in the story.

Now you've created your own hilarious MAD LIBS® game!

---

# GIRLS' NIGHT OUT

VERB _____

ANIMAL (PLURAL) _____

ADJECTIVE_____

ADJECTIVE_____

ADJECTIVE_____

NOUN _____

VERB _____

ADJECTIVE_____

PART OF THE BODY _____

ADJECTIVE_____

PLURAL NOUN _____

NOUN _____

NOUN _____

# MAD LIBS®
# GIRLS' NIGHT OUT

Sometimes you just want to _____ with your

_VERB_

girlfriends without having to fend off _____ all

_ANIMAL (PLURAL)_

night—particularly after going through a/an _____

_ADJECTIVE_

breakup. You're just not up to creating _____ responses

_ADJECTIVE_

to _____ one-liners. Well, the truth is that most

_ADJECTIVE_

men are intimidated by women, and if you give off the right

_____, they'll _____ away from you.

_NOUN_ _VERB_

Follow these tips to enjoy your _____ girls' night out

_ADJECTIVE_

uninterrupted:

- Don't make lingering _____ contact.

  _PART OF THE BODY_

- Opt out of the _____ contests.

  _ADJECTIVE_

- Don't allow the _____ to dance too close.

  _PLURAL NOUN_

- Resist the urge to dance on top of the _____.

  _NOUN_

- Keep yourself from yelling, "Who's going to buy me a/an

_____!"

_NOUN_

From ADVICE FOR THE LOVELORN MAD LIBS® • Copyright © 2005 by Chamberlain Bros.,
a division of Penguin Group (USA), Inc., 375 Hudson Street, New York, New York 10014.

MAD LIBS® is fun to play with friends, but you can also play it by yourself! To begin with, DO NOT look at the story on the page below. Fill in the blanks on this page with the words called for. Then, using the words you have selected, fill in the blank spaces in the story.

Now you've created your own hilarious MAD LIBS® game!

# A DOUBLE WHAMMY

ADJECTIVE_____

NUMBER _____

ADJECTIVE_____

PLURAL NOUN _____

PART OF THE BODY_____

ADVERB_____

ADJECTIVE_____

ARTICLE OF CLOTHING_____

ADVERB_____

SILLY WORD_____

SAME SILLY WORD _____

ADJECTIVE_____

ADJECTIVE_____

ANIMAL _____

VERB _____

PLURAL NOUN _____

VERB _____

ADJECTIVE_____

# MAD LIBS®
# A DOUBLE WHAMMY

Dear Dating Diva,

I am such a/an _____ loser. My boyfriend of _____
            ADJECTIVE                                              NUMBER

months just left me for my _____ friend. I guess the
                                    ADJECTIVE

obvious _____ were all there: prolonged _____
         PLURAL NOUN                                      PART OF THE BODY

contact, the fact that he _____ invited her along on
                                    ADVERB

our_____ dates, and then there's the time I found her
      ADJECTIVE

_____ in his _____. Still, I'm feeling
ARTICLE OF CLOTHING          NOUN

_____ betrayed. How will I ever get over this?
     ADVERB

— _____
     SILLY WORD

Dear _____,
       SAME SILLY WORD

Of course you're feeling _____, but you're better off,
                                 ADJECTIVE

Believe me! She was not a very _____ friend. And he's
                                       ADJECTIVE

just proven himself to be a pretty stupid _____.
                                                   ANIMAL

_____ for a couple of days and then, for _____
     VERB                                                   PLURAL NOUN

sake _____ on with your _____ life.
        VERB                              ADJECTIVE

From ADVICE FOR THE LOVELORN MAD LIBS® • Copyright © 2005 by Chamberlain Bros., a division of Penguin Group (USA), Inc., 375 Hudson Street, New York, New York 10014.

MAD LIBS® is fun to play with friends, but you can also play it by yourself! To begin with, DO NOT look at the story on the page below. Fill in the blanks on this page with the words called for. Then, using the words you have selected, fill in the blank spaces in the story.

Now you've created your own hilarious MAD LIBS® game!

# MAKEOVER

NUMBER _____

VERB _____

PLURAL NOUN _____

ADJECTIVE _____

ADJECTIVE _____

PLURAL NOUN _____

CITY _____

CELEBRITY (FEMALE) _____

NOUN _____

VERB ENDING IN "ING" _____

ADJECTIVE _____

COLOR _____

COLOR _____

NOUN _____

ADJECTIVE _____

ADVERB _____

ADJECTIVE _____

ADVERB _____

ADJECTIVE _____

# MAD LIBS®
# MAKEOVER

It's been _____ months since the break-up and it's time
              NUMBER

to _____ out there again. How about a makeover to
       VERB

show your _____ you're not the same _____
         PLURAL NOUN              ADJECTIVE

girl anymore? First, remember that when it comes to cosmetics, less is

_____. "Too much makeup adds _____,
   ADJECTIVE                   PLURAL NOUN

makes you look older," according to one _____ make-up
                                CITY

artist, who works with _____. Instead of reaching for
                  CELEBRITY (FEMALE)

the _____ of years past, try _____
      NOUN                   VERB ENDING IN "ING"

products, which can brighten your _____ skin. The
                         ADJECTIVE

_____ and _____ hues can be mixed
    COLOR               COLOR

with your favorite _____ and applied to your skin to
               NOUN

ensure the _____ look you desire. But proceed
         ADJECTIVE

_____ because glittery makeup looks best on younger
   ADVERB

_____. Not that you're old but well, you're older than
  PLURAL NOUN

before he dumped you, and time stops for no _____.
                                    NOUN

Sorry!

From ADVICE FOR THE LOVELORN MAD LIBS® • Copyright © 2005 by Chamberlain Bros.,
a division of Penguin Group (USA), Inc., 375 Hudson Street, New York, New York 10014.

MAD LIBS® is fun to play with friends, but you can also play it by yourself! To begin with, DO NOT look at the story on the page below. Fill in the blanks on this page with the words called for. Then, using the words you have selected, fill in the blank spaces in the story.

Now you've created your own hilarious MAD LIBS® game!

## LET US COUNT THE WAYS

ANIMAL _____

VERB ENDING IN "ING" _____

ADJECTIVE _____

ADJECTIVE _____

VERB _____

PLURAL NOUN _____

ADJECTIVE _____

PLURAL NOUN _____

ADJECTIVE _____

CELEBRITY (FEMALE) _____

NOUN _____

PART OF THE BODY _____

ADJECTIVE _____

EXCLAMATION _____

ADVERB _____

ADJECTIVE _____

ADJECTIVE _____

# MAD LIBS®
# LET US COUNT THE WAYS

That guy was real _____. Instead of _____
                     ANIMAL                              VERB ENDING IN "ING"

around, reminiscing about all the _____ times you
                                   ADJECTIVE

had together, think of some of the _____ reasons you
                                    ADJECTIVE

don't want to _____ him, anymore.
               VERB

• He never sent you a dozen _____ on your birthday.
                             PLURAL NOUN

• His idea of a/an _____ evening was buying frozen
                   ADJECTIVE

_____ at a/an _____ market.
   PLURAL NOUN              ADJECTIVE

• He was obsessed with _____, and you know she
                        CELEBRITY (FEMALE)

wouldn't give him the time of _____.
                               NOUN

• His _____ was pretty _____.
       PART OF THE BODY              ADJECTIVE

• His greeting was always "_____!"
                           EXCLAMATION

• He didn't realize what a/an _____ _____
                               ADVERB            ADJECTIVE

gal he had!

• He is a/an _____ loser.
              ADJECTIVE

From ADVICE FOR THE LOVELORN MAD LIBS® • Copyright © 2005 by Chamberlain Bros.,
a division of Penguin Group (USA), Inc., 375 Hudson Street, New York, New York 10014.

MAD LIBS® is fun to play with friends, but you can also play it by yourself! To begin with, DO NOT look at the story on the page below. Fill in the blanks on this page with the words called for. Then, using the words you have selected, fill in the blank spaces in the story.

Now you've created your own hilarious MAD LIBS® game!

# DANCE THERAPY

ADJECTIVE_____

NOUN _____

NOUN _____

ADVERB_____

VERB _____

ADJECTIVE_____

NOUN _____

ADJECTIVE_____

NUMBER (PLURAL) _____

PART OF THE BODY (PLURAL) _____

ADJECTIVE_____

VERB _____

VERB _____

PART OF THE BODY _____

ADJECTIVE_____

PLURAL NOUN _____

ADJECTIVE_____

PLURAL NOUN _____

# MAD LIBS®
# DANCE THERAPY

Sometimes the cure for a/an _____ heart is to dance
ADJECTIVE

until the wee hours of the _____ with your girlfriends
NOUN

at a/an _____ club. Now that you're _____
NOUN                                              ADVERB

on the market, you'll need to _____ up on your dance
VERB

moves. Here are some _____ tips for boogying down—
ADJECTIVE

in your own _____ or in front of a/an _____
A PLACE                                              ADJECTIVE

crowd of _____:
PLURAL NOUN

• Rotate your _____ to the music, of course.
PART OF THE BODY (PLURAL)

• If you have _____ hair, _____ it with
ADJECTIVE                         VERB

all you've got—but don't get so dizzy that you _____.
VERB

• Be sure to move your _____ with purpose—flailing
PART OF THE BODY

is not attractive or _____.
ADJECTIVE

• Put your hands on your _____ to look ultra-_____.
PLURAL NOUN                              ADJECTIVE

In no time at all, you'll be attracting many _____.
PLURAL NOUN

From ADVICE FOR THE LOVELORN MAD LIBS® • Copyright © 2005 by Chamberlain Bros.,
a division of Penguin Group (USA), Inc., 375 Hudson Street, New York, New York 10014.

MAD LIBS® is fun to play with friends, but you can also play it by yourself! To begin with, DO NOT look at the story on the page below. Fill in the blanks on this page with the words called for. Then, using the words you have selected, fill in the blank spaces in the story.

Now you've created your own hilarious MAD LIBS® game!

# EVEN CELEBRITIES GET DUMPED

CELEBRITY (MALE) _____

NOUN _____

CITY _____

VERB _____

ADJECTIVE _____

NOUN _____

NOUN _____

VERB ENDING IN "ING" _____

CELEBRITY (FEMALE) _____

ADJECTIVE _____

ADVERB _____

NOUN _____

EXCLAMATION _____

ADVERB _____

CELEBRITY (FEMALE) _____

VERB ENDING IN "ING" _____

ADJECTIVE _____

# MAD LIBS®
# EVEN CELEBRITIES
# GET DUMPED

Dear _____ ,
CELEBRITY (MALE)

By the time you read this, I will be on my private _____ flying
NOUN

to _____ to _____ my new album. You
CITY                              VERB

_____ piece of _____! Check out page
ADJECTIVE                              NOUN

three in the new issue of _____ magazine. There you are,
NOUN

_____ with _____ at a/an _____
VERB ENDING IN "ING"        CELEBRITY (FEMALE)              ADJECTIVE

party! I knew you had fallen _____ in love with her
ADVERB

when I saw you do that passionate _____ scene last
NOUN

month. _____, we're through!
EXCLAMATION

_____ ,
ADVERB

_____
CELEBRITY (FEMALE)

PS—And don't even think of _____ up at my
VERB ENDING IN "ING"

_____ premiere next month!
ADJECTIVE

From ADVICE FOR THE LOVELORN MAD LIBS® • Copyright © 2005 by Chamberlain Bros.,
a division of Penguin Group (USA), Inc., 375 Hudson Street, New York, New York 10014.

MAD LIBS® is fun to play with friends, but you can also play it by yourself! To begin with, DO NOT look at the story on the page below. Fill in the blanks on this page with the words called for. Then, using the words you have selected, fill in the blank spaces in the story.

Now you've created your own hilarious MAD LIBS® game!

# A LITTLE CHEERING UP

ADJECTIVE _____

PART OF THE BODY _____

ADVERB _____

ANIMAL _____

EXCLAMATION _____

ADJECTIVE _____

ADJECTIVE _____

NOUN _____

VERB _____

PLURAL NOUN _____

ADVERB _____

OCCUPATION _____

ADJECTIVE _____

NOUN _____

NUMBER _____

VERB _____

# MAD LIBS®
# A LITTLE CHEERING UP

It's natural for you to be feeling a little _____ so soon
ADJECTIVE

after having your _____ broken so _____
PART OF THE BODY                                          ADVERB

by that clueless _____. _____! Now is
ANIMAL                        EXCLAMATION

not the time for you to forget how _____ you are. Let
ADJECTIVE

us remind you:

• You are so _____ that a/an _____
ADJECTIVE                                          NOUN

should be named after you!

• Men _____ all over their _____ when
VERB                                          PLURAL NOUN

you walk by!

• You are so _____ intelligent that you could easily be a
ADVERB

successful _____!
OCCUPATION

• Your wit is so _____ you could make a/an _____
ADJECTIVE                                          NOUN

double over with laughter!

• There are _____ guys out there who would _____
NUMBER                                          VERB

to be by your side!

From ADVICE FOR THE LOVELORN MAD LIBS® • Copyright © 2005 by Chamberlain Bros.,
a division of Penguin Group (USA), Inc., 375 Hudson Street, New York, New York 10014.

MAD LIBS® is fun to play with friends, but you can also play it by yourself! To begin with, DO NOT look at the story on the page below. Fill in the blanks on this page with the words called for. Then, using the words you have selected, fill in the blank spaces in the story.

Now you've created your own hilarious MAD LIBS® game!

---

# ANOTHER TRY?

ADVERB_____

ADJECTIVE_____

PLURAL NOUN _____

ADVERB_____

VERB _____

ANIMAL _____

VERB _____

ADJECTIVE_____

PLURAL NOUN _____

PART OF THE BODY _____

NOUN _____

# MAD LIBS
# ANOTHER TRY?

You're so _____ wonderful that it's bound to happen:
          ADVERB

A knock on your front door, and there he is, with his _____
                                                      ADJECTIVE

eyes and an armful of _____. He tells you he misses
                         PLURAL NOUN

you _____; he can't _____ without you. He
       ADVERB                    VERB

realizes he's made a complete _____ of himself and
                                   ANIMAL

wants to _____ back together. Do you love him still?
            VERB

Only you know the _____ answer, but just remember that
                      ADJECTIVE

only five _____ ago he _____ out on you
             PLURAL NOUN             VERB (PAST TENSE)

and broke your _____. Be sure you know whether
                  PART OF THE BODY

he really wants to get back together or if he's just looking for a place

to hang his _____.
               NOUN

From ADVICE FOR THE LOVELORN MAD LIBS® • Copyright © 2005 by Chamberlain Bros.,
a division of Penguin Group (USA), Inc., 375 Hudson Street, New York, New York 10014.

MAD LIBS® is fun to play with friends, but you can also play it by yourself! To begin with, DO NOT look at the story on the page below. Fill in the blanks on this page with the words called for. Then, using the words you have selected, fill in the blank spaces in the story.

Now you've created your own hilarious MAD LIBS® game!

## BACK IN THE SADDLE

ADVERB _____

ADJECTIVE _____

NOUN _____

VERB _____

ADJECTIVE _____

PART OF THE BODY _____

TYPE OF FOOD _____

VERB ENDING IN "ING" _____

ADJECTIVE _____

NOUN _____

NOUN _____

NOUN _____

NOUN _____

VERB _____

ADJECTIVE _____

ADJECTIVE _____

NOUN _____

VERB ENDING IN "ING" _____

# MAD LIBS®
# BACK IN THE SADDLE

Sure, you've just been _____ burned by that
<br>ADVERB

_____ _____, but you just can't
<br>ADJECTIVE      NOUN

_____ around. You're not going to waste the most
<br>VERB

_____ years of your life by stuffing your _____
<br>ADJECTIVE           PART OF THE BODY

with _____ and _____ on your sofa every
<br>TYPE OF FOOD    VERB ENDING IN "ING"

night. Here are some really _____ tips to get you back
<br>ADJECTIVE

into the real _____:
<br>NOUN

• Volunteer at your neighborhood _____
<br>NOUN

• Join a locoal sports _____
<br>NOUN

• Adopt a pet _____
<br>NOUN

• _____ up a/an _____ new hobby
<br>VERB       ADJECTIVE

• Travel to a/an _____ far off _____
<br>ADJECTIVE     NOUN

• Go _____ with your girlfriends
<br>VERB ENDING IN "ING"

From ADVICE FOR THE LOVELORN MAD LIBS® • Copyright © 2005 by Chamberlain Bros.,
a division of Penguin Group (USA), Inc., 375 Hudson Street, New York, New York 10014.

MAD LIBS® is fun to play with friends, but you can also play it by yourself! To begin with, DO NOT look at the story on the page below. Fill in the blanks on this page with the words called for. Then, using the words you have selected, fill in the blank spaces in the story.

Now you've created your own hilarious MAD LIBS® game!

# KNOW YOUR TYPE
## PART ONE

NOUN _____

ADJECTIVE _____

NOUN _____

ADJECTIVE _____

VERB _____

ADJECTIVE _____

PLURAL NOUN _____

ADJECTIVE _____

NOUN _____

PLURAL NOUN _____

NOUN _____

ADJECTIVE _____

VERB _____

ADJECTIVE _____

ADJECTIVE _____

# MAD LIBS®
# KNOW YOUR TYPE
# PART ONE

Chances are you've known a few losers in your day. Here's a/an

_____ guide to help you decide who gets your _____ and who
                                         NOUN

_____ gets shown to the _____.
ADJECTIVE                          NOUN

• Artist: When this guy writes a/an _____ poem about
                                 ADJECTIVE

you or paints a flattering portrait of you, you'll _____ faster
                                          VERB

than ice cream on a/an _____ day. Warning: avoid
                         ADJECTIVE

"tortured" artists who still live with their _____.
                                 PLURAL NOUN

• Professional: This guy will overwhelm you with his _____
                                          ADJECTIVE

dedication to his _____—not to mention his well-
                        NOUN

tailored _____. Warning: He can spend too many
                 PLURAL NOUN

hours at a/an place instead of at your gorgeous side.

• Hipster: Very trendy, this guy will take you to the most

_____ spots in town where you'll _____
ADJECTIVE                                       VERB

about the '80s. Warning: will probably have a/an _____
                                        ADJECTIVE

ego and a/an _____ wardrobe that puts yours to shame.
              ADJECTIVE

From ADVICE FOR THE LOVELORN MAD LIBS® • Copyright © 2005 by Chamberlain Bros.,
a division of Penguin Group (USA), Inc., 375 Hudson Street, New York, New York 10014.

MAD LIBS® is fun to play with friends, but you can also play it by yourself! To begin with, DO NOT look at the story on the page below. Fill in the blanks on this page with the words called for. Then, using the words you have selected, fill in the blank spaces in the story.

Now you've created your own hilarious MAD LIBS® game!

---

## WWW.INTERNETDATINGADVERTISEMENT.COM

ADJECTIVE_____

NOUN _____

NOUN _____

ADJECTIVE_____

ADJECTIVE_____

ADJECTIVE_____

NOUN _____

ADJECTIVE_____

NOUN _____

NOUN _____

PLURAL NOUN _____

PLURAL NOUN _____

PLURAL NOUN _____

ADJECTIVE_____

NOUN _____

# MAD LIBS®

## WWW.INTERNETDATINGADVERTISEMENT.COM

Tired of meeting _____ men in bars, _____
           ADJECTIVE                                      NOUN

parties or the _____ store? You're not alone. That's
                      NOUN

why today, many _____ women are using the Internet to find
                     ADJECTIVE

their _____ man. We at www.golden_____.com
       ADJECTIVE                                NOUN

will use our _____-tested, system for matching you
                    NOUN

with the _____ of your dreams based on your shared
               NOUN

values regarding _____ , _____, and
                      PLURAL NOUN          PLURAL NOUN

_____. Our method is so _____ that
     PLURAL NOUN                              ADJECTIVE

we guarantee you'll have a/an _____on your finger in
                                       NOUN

no time!

From ADVICE FOR THE LOVELORN MAD LIBS® • Copyright © 2005 by Chamberlain Bros.,
a division of Penguin Group (USA), Inc., 375 Hudson Street, New York, New York 10014.

MAD LIBS® is fun to play with friends, but you can also play it by yourself! To begin with, DO NOT look at the story on the page below. Fill in the blanks on this page with the words called for. Then, using the words you have selected, fill in the blank spaces in the story.

Now you've created your own hilarious MAD LIBS® game!

# KNOW YOUR TYPE
# PART TWO

VERB _____

NOUN _____

VERB ENDING IN "ING" _____

PART OF THE BODY (PLURAL) _____

ADJECTIVE_____

CELEBRITY (FEMALE) _____

NOUN _____

NOUN _____

ADJECTIVE_____

VERB ENDING IN "ING" _____

NOUN _____

PART OF THE BODY (PLURAL) _____

ADJECTIVE_____

ANIMAL _____

VERB ENDING IN "ING" _____

ADJECTIVE_____

PLURAL NOUN _____

ADJECTIVE_____

# MAD LIBS®
# KNOW YOUR TYPE
# PART TWO

• Athlete: Whether you _____ this guy at the gym, a
                                        VERB

sports _____, or _____ in the park,
              NOUN                    VERB ENDING IN "ING"

you'll be impressed by his killer _____. Warning:
                                    PART OF THE BODY (PLURAL)

if in time you discover a/an _____ poster of
                                      ADJECTIVE

_____ hanging over his _____ don't be surprised.
CELEBRITY (FEMALE)                        NOUN

• Environmentalist: This guy will woo you with his

_____ and a really _____ commitment to
        NOUN                          ADJECTIVE

_____ the planet. He will certainly be happy if you
VERB ENDING IN "ING"

don't wear a/an fur _____ or don't shave your
                            NOUN

_____. Warning: may be in need of a long,
PART OF THE BODY (PLURAL)

_____ shower.
      ADJECTIVE

• Geek: Having been the under-_____ for so long, this
                                        ANIMAL

guy is usually very _____ and sensitive. He probably
                      VERB ENDING IN "ING"

spent his adolescence _____, so he is probably
                              VERB ENDING IN "ING"

_____ and successful. Warning: may not have many
      ADJECTIVE

_____ and may be in need of a/an _____ makeover.
PLURAL NOUN                                        ADJECTIVE

From ADVICE FOR THE LOVELORN MAD LIBS® • Copyright © 2005 by Chamberlain Bros.,
a division of Penguin Group (USA), Inc., 375 Hudson Street, New York, New York 10014.

MAD LIBS® is fun to play with friends, but you can also play it by yourself! To begin with, DO NOT look at the story on the page below. Fill in the blanks on this page with the words called for. Then, using the words you have selected, fill in the blank spaces in the story.

Now you've created your own hilarious MAD LIBS® game!

# BEWARE THE FREAKS!

ADJECTIVE_____

ADJECTIVE_____

VERB ENDING IN "ING" _____

PART OF THE BODY (PLURAL) _____

VERB _____

ADJECTIVE_____

NOUN _____

ADVERB_____

ADVERB_____

SAME ADVERB _____

NOUN _____

ADJECTIVE_____

# MAD LIBS®
# BEWARE THE FREAKS!

Dear Dating Diva,

I really need some _____ advice. This _____
_____ADJECTIVE_____ ADJECTIVE

guy and I were _____ last week when I discovered
VERB ENDING IN "ING"

he has three _____! At first I thought I could
PART OF THE BODY (PLURAL)

_____ with it, but now I just think it's really _____.
VERB                                                      ADJECTIVE

He's called me several times since the incident, asking me out on

another _____. I'm _____ lonely.
NOUN                              ADVERB

Should I try to get over this?

_____ Confused
ADVERB

Dear _____ Confused,
SAME ADVERB

You should see a professional _____ about this
NOUN

_____ problem.
ADJECTIVE

From ADVICE FOR THE LOVELORN MAD LIBS® • Copyright © 2005 by Chamberlain Bros.,
a division of Penguin Group (USA), Inc., 375 Hudson Street, New York, New York 10014.

MAD LIBS® is fun to play with friends, but you can also play it by yourself! To begin with, DO NOT look at the story on the page below. Fill in the blanks on this page with the words called for. Then, using the words you have selected, fill in the blank spaces in the story.

Now you've created your own hilarious MAD LIBS® game!

# WHAT TO DO?

ADJECTIVE_____

NUMBER _____

ADJECTIVE_____

VERB ENDING IN "ING" _____

NOUN _____

NUMBER _____

ADJECTIVE_____

VERB _____

ADJECTIVE_____

PLURAL NOUN _____

ADJECTIVE_____

VERB _____

ADJECTIVE_____

CITY _____

SAME ADJECTIVE _____

SAME CITY_____

VERB _____

# MAD LIBS®
# WHAT TO DO?

Dear Dating Diva,

Help! I've been seeing this _____ guy for
ADJECTIVE

_____ weeks, and everything was _____
NUMBER                                                ADJECTIVE

until last week. We were talking about _____ on
VERB ENDING IN "ING"

a/an _____ together, when he told me he's seeing
NOUN

_____ other women, some of whom are quite _____!
NUMBER                                                ADJECTIVE

I really want to _____ this guy—he's really very
VERB

_____ and buys me lots of _____.
ADJECTIVE                                              PLURAL NOUN

I'm just not sure I can get past his _____ confession.
ADJECTIVE

How should I _____ this?
VERB

— _____ in _____
ADJECTIVE              CITY

Dear _____ in _____,
SAME ADJECTIVE          SAME CITY

Three words: _____ him, immediately!
VERB

From ADVICE FOR THE LOVELORN MAD LIBS® • Copyright © 2005 by Chamberlain Bros.,
a division of Penguin Group (USA), Inc., 375 Hudson Street, New York, New York 10014.

# Adult
# MAD LIBS®
## World's Greatest Word Game
### Roger Price and Leonard Stern

**L**ook for these other fun Adult Mad Libs® titles at a bookseller near you!

## ADVICE FOR THE LOVELORN

Dumper? Dumpee? Who's sorry now? This compilation of advice column wisdom, Dear John letters, old love notes, and other comforts is for those tortured souls left in the lurch, whose friends simply don't want to hear about it anymore.

## KEEPERS AND LOSERS

A rating guide of men: smarts, looks, stamina, charm, manners, and other lists to rate whether you bring him home to Mom or throw him back into the sea.

## TEST YOUR RELATIONSHIP I.Q.

Take the tests and find out if you're a match made in heaven…or doomed to a life of utter boredom and marital horror!

## PARTY GIRL

Drink recipes, pickup lines, turndown lines, chick checklists, and more.